The Christmas Magic-Wagon

A Play

By June Behrens

Pictures by

Marjorie Burgeson

A Golden Gate Junior Book
Childrens Press, Chicago

Library of Congress Cataloging in Publication Data

Behrens, June.
   The Christmas magic-wagon.

   "A Golden Gate junior book."
   SUMMARY: A play in which the Jason family receives
back more than they give when they decide to make
Christmas a little brighter for the less fortunate families
along their road.
   1. Christmas plays. [1. Christmas plays.
2. Plays] I. Burgeson, Marjorie. II. Title.
PN6120.C5B46 812'.5'4 75-14007
ISBN 0-516-08880-7

1 2 3 4 5 6 7 8 9 10 11 12 R 78 77 76 75

Characters

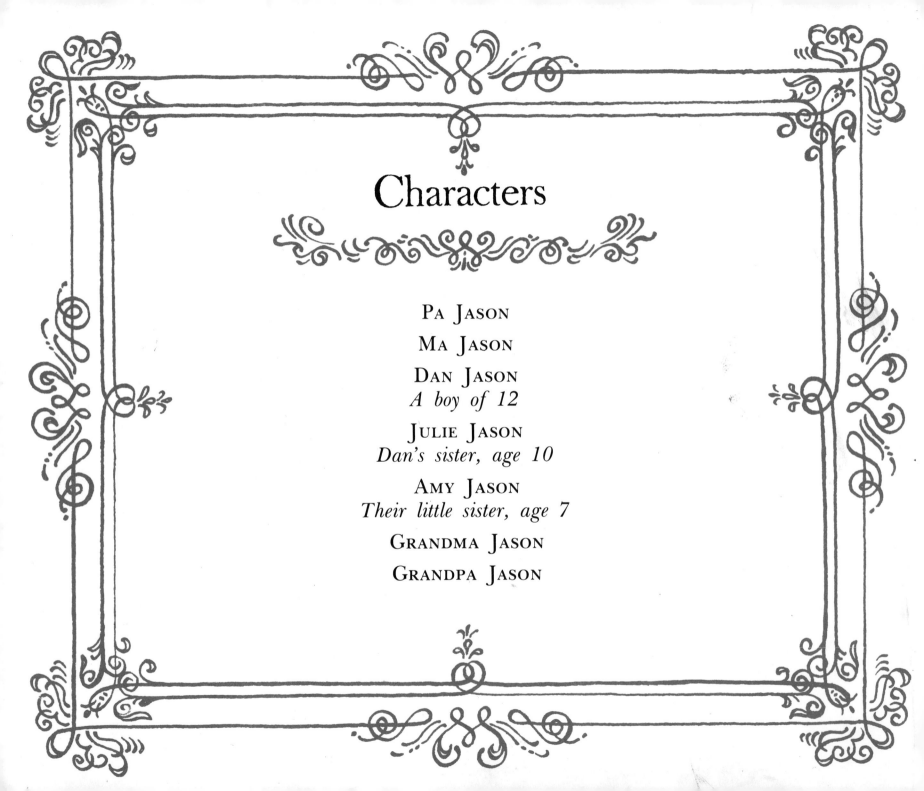

PA JASON

MA JASON

DAN JASON
A boy of 12

JULIE JASON
Dan's sister, age 10

AMY JASON
Their little sister, age 7

GRANDMA JASON

GRANDPA JASON

PA   MA   DAN   JULIE   AMY   GRANDMA   GRANDPA

ACT I

Home of the Jason family in the little town of Parkville
December 1900

SETTING AT RISE OF CURTAIN:

A large living room-kitchen behind the general store.

MA: Grandpa and the children have been out in the woods all afternoon looking for our Christmas tree. I declare, they should have found one by now.

GRANDMA: You know Grandpa. He won't cut down just any tree. It has to be exactly the right one. And all three children will have to have their say. It can take a time to find a tree that will please them all.

(Enter Pa)

PA: Aren't Grandpa and the kids home yet?

MA: They're taking their time. They know there won't be much Christmas spirit in Parkville this year, so the tree has to be extra-special.

PA: I closed the store early. Not many folks came around today. It has been a bad year for everyone, and that flood last month didn't help any.

GRANDMA: Parkville folks will make do with what they have this Christmas.

MA: Is that our wagon coming? It is! I can hear that squeaky wheel. Pa, put another stick of wood in the stove. Those young ones will be blue with cold.

GRANDMA: Butter and honey with hot bread will help take off the chill.

(Enter Amy)

AMY: Wait till you see our Christmas tree! It's the best one we've ever had!

(Enter Grandpa and Dan, pulling a large tree through the door. Julie follows. They set up the tree near the window.)

GRANDPA: It took a deal of looking, but we found a beauty.

GRANDMA: That's the prettiest tree we've had for many a Christmas.

DAN: I smell fresh bread. Ma, is it ready yet?

MA: Grandma, you set up the table while I get these young ones out of their heavy things.

GRANDMA: How far did you have to go to get a tree that big?

JULIE: We went all the way up to the creek. We saw where the water flooded the houses on Gibson Road.

DAN: James lives out there and he says they're not going to have any Christmas at his house.

JULIE: James isn't the only one. What about Sara and Andy's family? They live on Gibson Road too.

GRANDPA: None of the folks out that way will have much Christmas.

PA: They come into the store to pick up the mail, but they're not buying much more than flour, a little sugar and a few supplies. It's real hard times for them.

AMY: Maybe they'll feel better if they find Christmas trees as pretty as ours. Come on, Julie. I can't wait to put on the decorations we made last night.

JULIE: Everyone must help decorate the tree. Pa and Grandpa, you'll have to reach the high places with the strings of popcorn and cranberries.

DAN: I wish we could do something special for James and his family.

JULIE: Don't forget Sara and Andy.

DAN: Do you think we could make a Christmas for them all?

PA: That's a good thought, Dan. We should think on it.

AMY: How can you make a Christmas?

JULIE: Well, Grandma always says that Christmas is a time when we should stop thinking so much about ourselves and start thinking about others.

MA: It's a time of hope for better things to come.

DAN: Christmas is a good time to make other people happy by doing something special for them. That's so they'll know you're their best friend.

AMY: But *how* can we make a Christmas for our friends on Gibson Road?

DAN: Well, when we make our gifts for each other, why couldn't we each make something extra...and...

JULIE: And Christmas Eve we could load up the wagon and take Christmas to everybody on Gibson Road!

GRANDMA: Now that's what Christmas is all about, Amy. It's the doing for and giving to others that *make* Christmas. And sometimes you end up getting more than you give.

DAN: How could that happen?

GRANDMA: Well, it's a sort of magic, I guess, but it's true enough. Maybe sometime you children will find out.

GRANDPA: Sounds like you kids have just put together a Christmas surprise for James and Sara and Andy. I think they'll find something in their stockings on Christmas morning after all.

PA: Young Dan, I can think of no better way of celebrating the birthday of Jesus. We'll load up the wagon and drive to Gibson Road on Christmas Eve for sure!

ACT II

Act II

Scene 1: Early Christmas Eve morning a week later. Ma, the three children and Grandma are busy wrapping gifts and getting food together to take to Gibson Road.

DAN: Ma, your peach preserves will be a treat for everyone in James' family.

MA: Here's a half dozen extra jars. We had some nice peaches last summer and I just kept right on canning. Now I know why.

GRANDMA: I had enough yarn to make two extra pairs of mittens and a muffler.

AMY: Just look at the little corn shuck dolls Julie made. I hope I'll get one in *my* stocking Christmas morning!

JULIE: Amy, those little pincushions you made could be used for doll pillows, too.

MA: Dan, let us see what you've been whittling on all week.

DAN: Oh, it's only a little old dog. James loves his dog, so I whittled out one that looks almost like Old Blue.

(Enter Grandpa)

GRANDPA: Here's a nice bucket of hickory nuts that will help fill some Christmas stockings. But the snow hasn't let up for a minute. If it doesn't stop soon, we might not get out tonight.

DAN: Grandpa, don't even think that. Everything is ready. We've *got* to get to Gibson Road tonight!

(Enter Pa, carrying a bushel basket)

PA: These apples can go on the wagon. Grandpa, did Joe Smith get that wheel fixed and back on the wagon?

GRANDPA: Oh my, *I plumb forgot!* I meant to get back over to the blacksmith shop early this morning. Joe hadn't started to work on it last evening.

PA: We can't take that wagon out with one bad wheel in weather like this.

DAN: Pa, let me go over and see Mr. Smith. I'll bring home the wagon and it'll be ready to go. *(Hurries out before Pa can answer)*.

AMY: Ma, will we get to take the Christmas ride to see James and Sara and Andy?

MA: We'll wait and see, Amy. If the snow stops and if they can get that wheel fixed, everything will be all right.

Scene 2: Late afternoon.

MA: Children, it was a wonderful idea, wanting to make a Christmas for the folks on Gibson Road. But I guess it just wasn't meant to be.

JULIE: It isn't too late yet, is it, Pa?

AMY: The snow stopped hours ago.

PA: Well, it's getting late and Dan isn't back yet. If Joe Smith didn't have time enough to fix that wheel, there's no way to get out to Gibson Road tonight. I know you've all been busy making this Christmas for your friends. But don't feel too bad if it has to wait until another day.

AMY: But Christmas won't wait. It's here right now!

GRANDMA: Well, the idea of thinking about others is good all year round.

JULIE: But Grandma, that's not the same thing at all! Look! Here comes Dan. Listen to the sleigh bells on the wagon!

AMY: He's here! He's here!

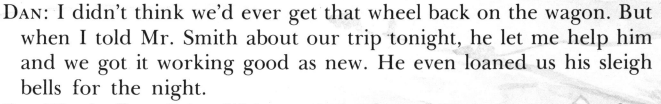

(Enter Dan)

DAN: I didn't think we'd ever get that wheel back on the wagon. But when I told Mr. Smith about our trip tonight, he let me help him and we got it working good as new. He even loaned us his sleigh bells for the night.

PA: That's fine, Dan. We're proud of you. Now get moving fast, everybody. Julie and Amy, get wrapped up good and warm. We'll load up the wagon.

GRANDPA: I'll fetch the lantern.

MA: Grandma and I will have apple pie and hot milk ready for you when you get home.

GRANDMA: While you're gone, we'll be getting that turkey ready to roast for Christmas dinner tomorrow. Wish all the folks on Gibson Road a Merry Christmas from Ma and me.

Scene 3: Later that night.
(Sound of returning sleigh bells. Enter the three children and Grandpa.)

MA: My goodness, you were gone a long time.

GRANDPA: We saw all the folks on Gibson Road.

(The children and Grandpa are strangely quiet as they remove caps, coats and mufflers.)

MA: I don't understand. When you left, you were all so excited and pleased with yourselves. Now you're as quiet and mysterious as can be.

GRANDMA: Amy, will you tell us what happened tonight?

AMY: Well, we turned down Gibson Road, and...

(Enter Pa)

PA: The horse and wagon's put away. Amy, have you told our story?

GRANDMA: We can't get a word out of anybody.

PA: No wonder. We can't tell you exactly what happened because we don't know.

GRANDPA: In all my years I've never seen anything like it.

MA: Like *what?* For goodness sakes, will somebody say something?

AMY: I'll tell you what happened. We think we rode in a *magic wagon* — an honest-to-goodness *magic wagon*...

27

MA: Child, what are you talking about, making up a story like that? And on this night.

PA: But she's right, Ma. Something happened that we don't understand.

DAN: We turned down Gibson Road and stopped to see James and his family. Their place is first on the road. We took in a big load of presents.

JULIE: Then we stopped at the next house, at Sara's. Everybody was so happy to see us. Sara's family didn't even have a Christmas tree.

GRANDPA: When we climbed back in the wagon the back end was *still* full of nuts and apples.

PA: We thought we couldn't have brought *that* much.

AMY: It was like that all the way down Gibson Road! We stopped at every house and left something. We helped make Christmas for every one of those flooded-out families.

PA: And Ma — *that wagon never did empty out.*

DAN: After the third stop we found a great big bundle of firewood in the wagon. And when we came away from visiting the Watson family — would you believe it? — there was a big holly wreath on top of the wood!

JULIE: We knew by then that there *must* be something magic about our wagon.

DAN: At the last house at the end of the road we scooped up everything we'd brought. The Hicks' have all those kids.

GRANDPA: Those folks were so glad to see us they just dragged us inside. We sampled Mrs. Hicks' gingersnaps and sang some Christmas songs and stayed quite a spell.

DAN: When we got back in the wagon to come home, we couldn't believe our eyes. That wagon was just about full up again! There was more holly and a big sack of pine cones. And on top of everything was a little Christmas tree!

PA: When we turned around and came back up the road on our way home, all the families came out of their houses when they heard our sleigh bells. They all waved and called out Merry Christmas.

JULIE: It was the most wonderful Christmas Eve! We made Christmas for a lot of folks…and somebody made Christmas for us.

GRANDMA: It's not too surprising. It's like I told you about giving and doing for others. Something magic happens when you give from the heart — *with no thought of getting anything back.* Don't ever forget how your Christmas Eve ride became a magic-wagon ride. I believe in magic-wagons. I've always believed.

It was almost Christmas. The three Jason children were helping Grandpa set up the Christmas tree in a corner of the family living room-kitchen behind Pa's general store when the Big Idea came to them. Times had been hard in the little town of Parkville that year of 1900. A flood had brought suffering to many families and the children knew that many of their friends wouldn't even have a Christmas tree, let alone any presents. It was Dan, the oldest, who proposed making the extra gifts and from there it was easy to evolve a plan for loading up the wagon on Christmas Eve to "take Christmas" to all the families who weren't going to have any. How all the Jasons entered into the project (which, they found, was not without its difficulties) and how, in the end, the children learned that something magic happens when one gives from the heart, climaxes a play that goes straight to the core of Christmas. *The Christmas Magic-Wagon* can be easily acted out or simply read for the story itself. Marjorie Burgeson's charming turn-of-the-century drawings in full color add a pleasantly nostalgic note.

JUNE BEHRENS is the author of two previous plays for children, *Feast Of Thanksgiving* and *A New Flag For A New Country,* published by Childrens Press. She has also written a number of books for young readers on an astonishing variety of subjects, from *Soo Ling Finds A Way,* the story of a little Chinese-American girl (a Junior Literary Guild selection) to the *True Book Of Metric Measurement.* A well-known educator, Mrs. Behrens (who is listed in *Who's Who In American Women)* is a reading specialist in one of California's largest public school systems. She spent her undergraduate days at the University of California at Santa Barbara, then earned her Master's degree in Administration from the University of Southern California. She and her husband make their home in the pleasant seaside town of Redondo Beach near Los Angeles.

MARJORIE BURGESON is a painter, sculptor and graphics designer who has won many honors for her work. A resident of Southern California (she lives with her husband and two daughters in the college community of Claremont), her drawings and sculptures have been exhibited at the Los Angeles County Museum of Art, the San Diego Fine Arts Gallery, the San Francisco Museum of Art, and in a number of private galleries. Mrs. Burgeson attended Scripps College where she majored in art, then went on to obtain a Master's degree in Fine Arts from Claremont Graduate School. At both institutions she won scholarships and a number of awards. For more than a dozen years she has designed toys and has found time to teach art classes for both children and adults.